Based on the Song 'Ōpae Ē by Pilahi Pākī and Irm

'Ōpae Ē

The Story

English-Version by Raymond Kaimana Estrella
and Jenny Moanikeala Estrella
Illustrations by Jenny Moanikeala Estrella

Introduction
By Raymond Kaimana Estrella

ʻŌpae Ē is a song written by Pilahi Pākī with music composed by Irmgard Farden Aluli. This song speaks of a young boy of Kahakuloa, Maui, who seeks to rescue his sister from a large eel. Along the way he meets various sea creatures and asks for their help. Only the bravest of these creatures will join him in his attempt to save his sister.

The English Version of this story is not an exact translation from the Hawaiian words found in the song, however, it was retold to incorporate a wider array of vocabulary for the budding student.

Words to the song 'Ōpae Ē by Pilahi Pākī
and Irmgard Farden Aluli

The 'Ōpae Ē story as retold by
Jenny Moanikeala Estrella and
Raymond Kaimana Estrella

ʻŌpae ē, ʻŌpae hoʻi.
Ua hele mai au,
ua hele mai au
na kuahine.

Ai iā wai?

"Little ʻŌpae, little ʻŌpae, please help. I have come because I need to rescue my sister."

"Where is she?" asked the little ʻŌpae.

Ai iā Puhi.

"Puhi has captured her! Will you help me?" Begged the brother.

Nui ʻo Puhi a liʻiliʻi au.
ʻAʻole loa!

"Puhi is so big and I am so small. No ways,
I cannot help you," said the ʻŌpae.

Still looking for help, the worried little brother
went to find someone else.

Pipipi ē, Pipipi hoʻi.
Ua hele mai au,
ua hele mai au
na kuahine.

Ai iā wai?
Ai iā Puhi.

"Tiny Pipipi, tiny Pipipi, please help. I need to rescue my sister."

"Where is she?" asked the tiny Pipipi.

"Puhi has taken her, can you help?"

Nui ʻo Puhi a liʻiliʻi au.
ʻAʻole loa!

"Puhi is so big and I am so small. No ways,
I cannot help you," said the Pipipi.

Sad, but not discouraged, the little brother kept
searching for help.

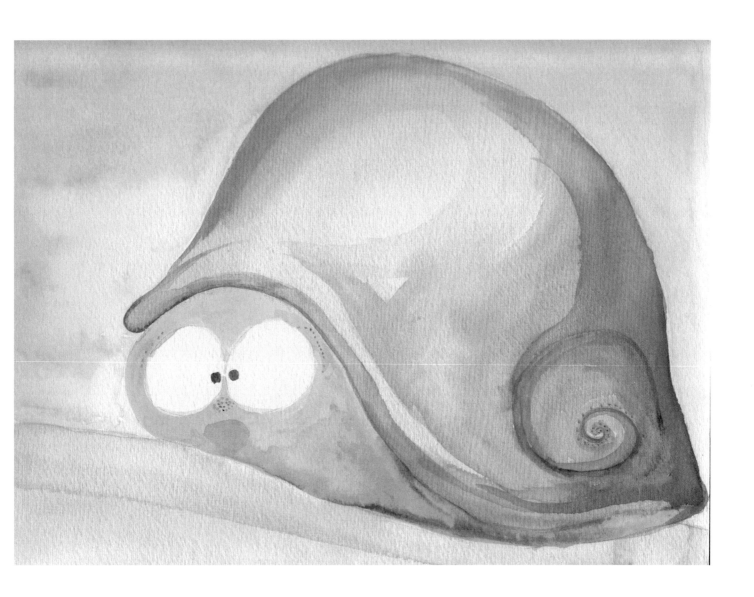

Pūpū ē, Pūpū hoʻi.
Ua hele mai au,
ua hele mai au
na kuahine.

Ai iā wai?
Ai iā Puhi.

"Small Pūpū, small Pūpū, please help. I need to rescue my sister."

"Where is she?" asked the small Pūpū .

"Puhi has taken her. Can you help?"

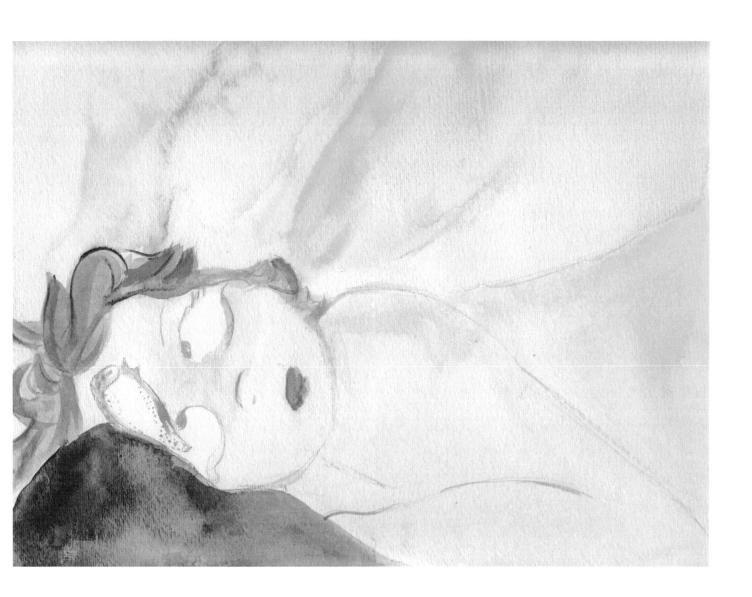

Nui ʻo Puhi a liʻiliʻi au.
ʻAʻole loa!

"Puhi is so big and I am so small. No ways, I cannot help you," said the Pūpū.

Despite not being able to find assistance the little brother trekked foward to find help.

Kūpeʻe ē, Kūpeʻe hoʻi.
Ua hele mai au,
ua hele mai au
na kuahine.

Ai iā wai?
Ai iā Puhi.

"Beautiful Kūpeʻe, beautiful Kūpeʻe, please help. I need to rescue my sister."

"Where is she?" asked the beautiful Kūpeʻe .

"Puhi has taken her, can you help?"

Nui ʻo Puhi a liʻiliʻi au.
ʻAʻole loa!

"Puhi is so big and I am so small. No ways, I cannot help you," said Kūpeʻe.

Hoping to find someone to help him he continued.

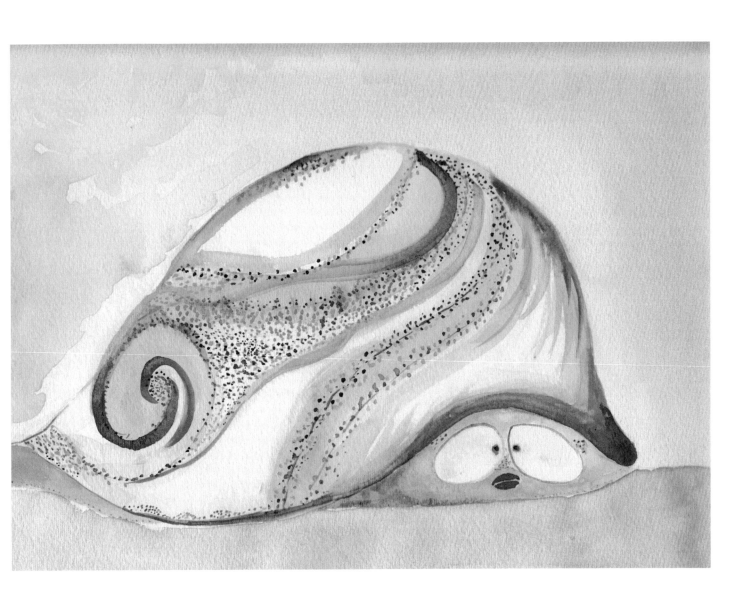

‘Opihi ē, ‘Opihi ho‘i.
Ua hele mai au,
ua hele mai au
na kuahine.

Ai iā wai?
Ai iā Puhi.

"Wise ‘Opihi, wise ‘Opihi, please help. I need to rescue my sister."

"Where is she?" asked the wise ‘Opihi.

"Puhi has taken her, can you help?"

19

Mai maka'u.

"The Puhi is big and I am small. But do not fear . . .
I will help you," said the fearless 'Opihi.

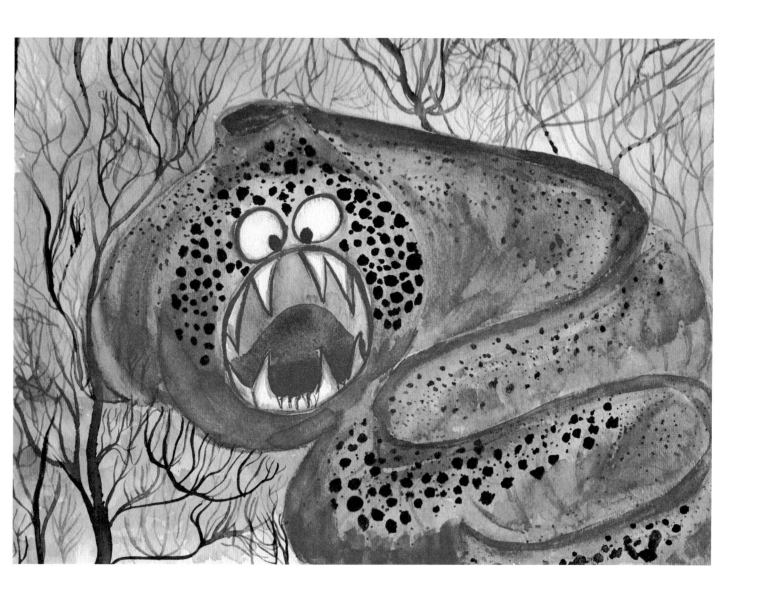

Na'u e pani
i ka maka a 'ike 'ole
kēlā puhi.

"I will cover his eyes and he will be blind. Then you can rescue your sister!"

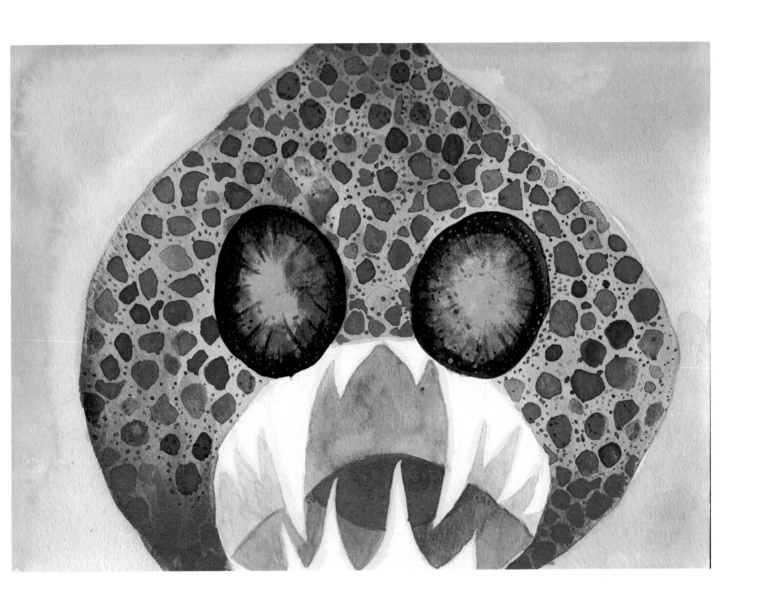

24

"Wiwo 'ole ka 'Opihi. You are the bravest. Mahalo nui for helping us," said the little boy and his sister.

For more fun visit Halepili.com
to download a free copy of
our companion workbook for this story.

Other Halepili Publications

Ku'u I'a 'Ewalu Ona Lima
(My Fish with Eight Legs)

He'e and 'Iole
(Octopus and Rat)
English Version

He'e and 'Iole
Hawaiian Version

halepili
homemade in hawaii

*H*alepili is a family that decided to embark on a journey of passion.   Exploring and learning through moʻolelo and the knowledge of our ancestors while learning to express and sustain ourselves through art and homemade ʻike-based products. This thirst for adventure carved out an environment that has supported our family growth. One of our greatest passions being the sharing of our moʻolelo through puppet shows to strengthen our pilina me ʻoukou. Feel free to contact us through halepili.com, we would love to expand our personal hale pili, an original Hawaiian schoolhouse, with all our ʻohana ma kēia honua nei.

Made in the USA
Columbia, SC
09 March 2019